Dawn of the Garden

In the hush of morning's light,
The petals whisper dreams in flight,
Golden rays awake the dew,
As day embraces earth anew.

Butterflies on gentle wings,
Flutter where the robin sings,
A tapestry of colors bright,
In this canvas, pure delight.

The sun ascends, a fiery crown,
Chasing shadows from the town,
Each bud unfurls with softest grace,
In the garden's warm embrace.

Awake now, the world aligns,
Nature's palette intertwines,
With every breath, a vibrant tune,
In the dawn, the flowers bloom.

Awakening Earth

Beneath the frost, the seeds still dream,
Awaiting the sun's gentle gleam,
Whispers of soil softly rise,
In the heart of winter's sighs.

As crocus peek from blankets white,
Emerging from the longest night,
The world is sculpted by rebirth,
In the warmth of awakening earth.

Rivers thaw and babble low,
Hearts of trees begin to glow,
A symphony of life unfurled,
In the cradle of the world.

The winds caress the eager prairies,
Awakening ancient canopies,
In every corner, nature stirs,
As hope within the season purrs.

Fertile Futures

From the depths of loamy grace,
New beginnings find their place,
Beneath the surface, roots entwine,
In silent promise, futures shine.

Hands that toil on sacred ground,
With every seed, new dreams are found,
As laughter echoes through the rows,
A testament of love that grows.

The garden hums, a vibrant space,
Where life and hope embrace their pace,
With every bloom, a tale retold,
Fertile futures, brave and bold.

In the heart of nature's scheme,
We sow the whispers of a dream,
For every flower, a chance reborn,
In fields of green, we find the morn.

The Blooming Odyssey

In gardens lush where stories dance,
A journey sparked by chance romance,
Petals unfurl like sails divine,
In this blooming odyssey, intertwined.

From bud to blossom, colors change,
Life's canvas, vast and strange,
With every scent, a memory made,
In the vibrant tapestry we've laid.

The sun dips low, the shadows creep,
While creatures stir from slumber deep,
A nightly glow, the stars conspiring,
In the garden, hearts are desiring.

Through every season's sweet embrace,
We wander realms of time and space,
In every petal's soft caress,
The odyssey blooms, we are blessed.

Rise and Flourish

In the morning's gentle glow, we rise,
With the sun's warmth kissing our open eyes.
Through shadows of doubt, we find our way,
Embracing the promise of a brand new day.

With roots entwined deep in the earth,
We push towards the sky, celebrating our birth.
Each dream a petal, adorned with care,
In the garden of life, we're destined to share.

Declarations of Dawn

Whispers of light spill over the hills,
As dawn breaks softly, the world it fills.
Colors awaken, vibrant and bright,
A canvas unfurling, hearts take flight.

Each moment a gem, a treasure to seize,
Nature's orchestra plays, a symphony of ease.
With courage ignited, we step into chance,
In the dance of the dawn, we're entranced.

The Palette of Blossoms

Petals unfurl in a riot of hues,
Each flower a story, each fragrance a muse.
From whispers of pink to bold crimson flair,
The garden's a canvas of love and care.

Bees hum a tune, weaving dew into dreams,
As sunlight cascades in golden beams.
In nature's embrace, we find our own tune,
Painting our lives beneath the watchful moon.

Awakening Dreams

In the silence of night, dreams softly gleam,
Stirring the heart with a whispered theme.
Stars weave their magic, a tapestry bright,
Guiding our souls through the restless night.

As dawn's first light breaks the spell of the dark,
Hope flares anew, igniting a spark.
With visions ignited, we rise and we soar,
Awakening dreams, forever in store.

Boisterous Breezes

The wind dances through the trees,
Whistling secrets, carrying ease.
It lifts the leaves on high, so bright,
A melody of nature, pure delight.

Through fields of gold, it sweeps and swirls,
Playful whispers from distant worlds.
With every gust, it sings and spins,
In boisterous laughter, life begins.

Roots and Wings

Beneath the soil, the roots entwine,
Holding stories, aged like wine.
They grasp the earth with patient grace,
While dreams of flight whisper in space.

From sturdy roots, the branches soar,
Reaching heights they've longed for.
The heart is anchored, yet yearns to roam,
In harmony, both wings and roots find home.

Celebrating the Thaw

As frost retreats, the world awakes,
A symphony of life, the earth remakes.
Bud and bloom, in vibrant praise,
Celebrate the warmth of sunlit days.

With each drop of thaw, the laughter flows,
Through meadows green where the wildflower
grows.
Nature's canvas, bright and bold,
In winter's wake, a story unfolds.

Rhapsody of Colors

In a painter's dream, the hues collide,
A rhapsody of colors, a joyful ride.
Crimson sunsets and azure skies,
Whisper stories in their vibrant ties.

Golden tints on dusky wings,
Nature's palette celebrates all things.
With every brushstroke, life transcends,
In this vivid symphony, joy never ends.

Melody of Growth

Beneath the earth, the seeds do stir,
Whispering dreams where roots confer.
In silent depths, the world awakes,
With tender hearts, the green life breaks.

Each gentle shoot, a song anew,
A symphony in morning dew.
As sunlight paints the leaves in gold,
The melody of growth unfolds.

Sprouts of Hope

In cracks of stone, the flowers rise,
Defying fate, they touch the skies.
With every bloom, a story told,
Of perseverance, brave and bold.

From shadows deep, they find the light,
Sprouts of hope in day and night.
Each petal soft, a sigh released,
A testament of life increased.

Laughter in the Breeze

The wind carries laughter through the trees,
A playful dance, a gentle tease.
With every sigh, the branches sway,
As nature hums, in bright array.

Children's giggles blend with the air,
In fields of gold, without a care.
Moments cherished, joy's embrace,
Life's sweet song in time and space.

Vibrant Horizons

Beneath the canvas of dawn's array,
Vibrant horizons greet the day.
With colors bright, the sky ignites,
Painting dreams in morning lights.

Every step on this fertile ground,
Whispers of wonders yet to be found.
Together we chase the fading night,
In vibrant horizons, hearts take flight.

Awakening the Soul

In the quiet dawn when shadows flee,
The whispering breeze speaks tenderly,
Soft daylight spills on the sleeping earth,
A promise of hope, a moment of rebirth.

Each heartbeat echoes a gentle call,
Reviving dreams that once felt small,
Embracing the warmth of a new day's light,
The soul emerges, ready to take flight.

The Garden's Secret

Deep in the garden where wildflowers grow,
Lies a secret hidden from the world's flow,
Petals unfurl in colors divine,
Whispering wisdom in silence, they shine.

Among tangled roots and dewdrops bright,
Lives a magic that dances in soft twilight,
Nature's embrace, both gentle and bold,
In the heart of the garden, stories unfold.

Whispers of Rejuvenation

As twilight descends, the stars come alive,
Soft murmurs of night begin to revive,
Moonlight spills secrets on paths yet untold,
Inviting the weary to let go and unfold.

In the coolness of dusk, old burdens take flight,
The soul finds its solace in the soft, tranquil light,

Like the coming of spring in the heart of the frost,

Rejuvenation whispers, no moment is lost.

A Tapestry of Growth

In the tapestry woven with colors so bright,
Threads of experience, joy mixed with plight,
Each stitch a memory, a lesson, a dream,
Together they flourish, a beautiful theme.

Roots dive deep while branches reach high,
Nature's design under the vast, starry sky,
With each passing season, the story adds grace,
In life's grand mosaic, we all find our place.

The Firefly's Hope

In twilight's embrace, where shadows play,
Glows a flicker of light, drifting away.
A dance in the dark, a whisper of dreams,
Guiding lost souls through moonlit beams.

With fragile wings, it weaves through the night,
A beacon of hope, a spark of delight.
Though storms may rage and the skies turn gray,
The firefly's glow will lead the way.

Odes to Renewal

As springtime arrives with a delicate sigh,
The world wakes anew, beneath a vast sky.
Petals unfurl, in colors so bright,
A promise of warmth, in the soft morning light.

From ashes of winter, the green shoots emerge,
Life dances again, in a glorious surge.
Each bloom is a chapter, each bud is a word,
The odes of renewal, in whispers unheard.

Pathways of Petals

Upon the soft earth, a carpet unfolds,
With whispers of stories from petals of gold.
Dancing in circles, the winds share their song,
Guiding us gently, where we all belong.

Through gardens of ink, and the fields of the past,

We walk hand in hand, on the memories cast.
In the fragrance of roses, the echoes reside,
Pathways of petals, where love cannot hide.

Joyful Returns

The sun greets the dawn with a radiant smile,
As laughter spills over, spanning a mile.
Children's hearts leap, as they dance in the rain,
In moments like these, all troubles are slain.

With friends by our side, we gather once more,
Through stories and songs, our spirits will soar.
For in every reunion, the world feels alive,
Joyful returns, where our dreams can thrive.

The Return of Green

In the embrace of spring's soft hand,
Nature awakens, a vibrant strand,
Emerald carpets grace the ground,
Whispers of life in every sound.

Leaves unfurl under the sun's warm gaze,
Buds burst forth in a lively craze,
Freshness dances on the gentle breeze,
A symphony played by swaying trees.

Gentle Thaw

Winter's grasp begins to yield,
Under sunlit arcs, the frost repealed,
Puddles glisten, a mirrored sky,
As nature stirs with a contented sigh.

Softly melting, a stream flows free,
Inviting whispers of what will be,
Awakening dreams from a frozen night,
In the heart of earth, hope ignites bright.

Petals Unfurled

In the garden's nook, a secret found,
Petals unfurl, colors abound,
Each blossom a story, fragrant and bold,
Whispering tales of love yet untold.

Butterflies flit in a playful dance,
Where silence blooms, and dreams entrance,
Every hue a symphony's part,
Crafting a masterpiece, a work of art.

When Earth Reclaims Color

With a sigh, the hues cascade,
As nature's palette begins to invade,
In cracked soil, the seeds find their way,
Painting the world in vibrant array.

Sunlight spills on forgotten paths,
Reviving stories of silent laughs,
When the earth awakens from shadow's blight,
Color returns, banishing night.

The Heartbeat of Flora

In the whisper of petals, secrets unfold,
A heartbeat of flora, in sunlit gold,
Gentle rustlings tell tales of the breeze,
As nature's soft symphony dances through trees.

Roots intertwine, a tapestry grand,
Connecting each story, touching the land,
With every moment, in shadows and light,
Flora's heartbeat pulses, a vibrant delight.

A Flourish of Life

Petals burst forth in colors so bright,
A flourish of life, waking from night,
With dew-kissed beginnings, each blossom will
rise,
Unfurling its beauty beneath endless skies.

In gardens of wonder where dreams intertwine,
Nature's paintbrush strokes with a rhythm divine,
From valleys to peaks, every hue sings,
A flourish of life through the joy that it brings.

Laughing Leaves

In the dance of the wind, where the laughter
resides,
Laughing leaves rustle, where joy never hides,
They twirl and they spin, in a jubilant flight,
Whispering secrets in the soft twilight.

Each leaf a storyteller, sharing delight,
Of summers long past and the stars in the night,
With every cascade, a memory weaves,
In the joyful embrace of the laughing leaves.

Hues of Expectation

In dawn's early blush, where the day starts to rise,
Hues of expectation paint across the skies,
With whispers of hope in a palette so bold,
Every moment unfolds, a story retold.

From whispers of lavender to golden embrace,
Each hue holds a promise, a time-worn grace,
To color our tomorrows with dreams yet unseen,
In the vibrant embrace of what might have been.

The Promise of Petals

In gardens bright where blossoms bloom,
A silent vow dispels the gloom.
Each petal whispers, soft and sweet,
A tale of hope beneath our feet.

With colors bold that brush the sky,
Each scent a hymn, a lullaby.
They dance in breezes, light and free,
A promise bound in tapestry.

The rain bestows a tender kiss,
Awakening life from evening's bliss.
With morning's light, their truth is seen,
A gentle world, in vibrant green.

So let us pause, and take a claim,
On petals' dreams, and love's sweet flame.
For in their hearts, we find our way,
In every dawn, in every fray.

Nature's Revival

As winter fades to spring's embrace,
The earth reclaims its vibrant space.
From barren ground to life anew,
A canvas rich with every hue.

The rivers sing of melting snow,
While gentle winds begin to blow.
The trees adorn in delicate lace,
Inviting joy, a warm embrace.

With every bud that starts to bloom,
We cast away the lingering gloom.
The chorus of the birds takes flight,
A symphony of pure delight.

In every corner, life will thrive,
Each heartbeat echoes, 'We survive.'
For nature's tale, a timeless spin,
Begins anew, where hope begins.

Unfurling Possibilities

Beneath the soil, the seeds await,
In silence kept, they contemplate.
Each droplet rains, a spark of fate,
To bring to life what hopes create.

With tender roots, they break the ground,
In shadows deep, their strength is found.
The sun bestows its golden rays,
To guide their dance in nature's plays.

In time, they stretch, and reach up high,
Each leaf a whisper to the sky.
With every branch that bends and sways,
Unfurling dreams in myriad ways.

So let us learn from every sprout,
That life's a dance, without a doubt.
In every turn, in every chance,
There lies a spark; there's always dance.

Morning's Gentle Embrace

Awake, the world begins to sigh,
With colors painting oceans shy.
Each ray of light, a soft caress,
In morning's arms, we find our rest.

The dewdrops glisten on the grass,
As whispers of the night will pass.
A symphony of peaceful sounds,
As nature stirs, and life abounds.

The sky alights in hues of gold,
A story of new morn unfolds.
With every breath, the day ignites,
In morning's warmth, our hope takes flight.

So take a moment, breathe it in,
The dawn unveils, as dreams begin.
With every heartbeat, every glance,
In morning's light, we find our chance.

Raindrop Serenade

Gentle whispers on the pane,
A melody that sweeps the plain.
Each drop a note, each splash a tune,
Dancing softly beneath the moon.

Puddles gather like dreams anew,
Reflecting skies of silver hue.
Nature's symphony fills the air,
In the rhythm of a raindrop's care.

Fields of Possibility

In the expanse where dreams take flight,
Golden grains kiss the warming light.
Each blade of grass, a tale untold,
A canvas vast, a heart of gold.

Winds whisper secrets of what might be,
The horizon calls with a voice so free.
In every corner, hope does reside,
Fields of possibility stretching wide.

Emerging Beauty

From the ash, the flower blooms,
Painting life in vibrant plumes.
Petals unfold with the morning light,
A testament to the enduring fight.

In every struggle, a story we find,
Emerging beauty, resilient and kind.
The world awakens with gentle grace,
Nature's embrace, our sacred place.

Breath of Fresh Air

Amidst the chaos, stillness calls,
A moment's pause, where silence falls.
Fresh air whispers through the trees,
A calming balm, a gentle breeze.

With every inhale, worries untwine,
In nature's embrace, the soul aligns.
Life's hurried pace, we learn to share,
Finding peace in the breath of fresh air.

Fertile Soil

In quiet depths where secrets lie,
Rich earth embraces dreams awry,
With tender roots that yearn to rise,
A symphony of life, the garden's guise.

Each grain a promise, every stone,
A testament to the seeds we've sown,
Through storms and sun, resilience shows,
In fertile soil, our spirit grows.

The Language of Bloom

Petals whisper stories soft and sweet,
In shades of hope, they gently greet,
Their colors dance on summer's breath,
A vivid tale of life and death.

Each blossom holds a secret rare,
Of fleeting time and lover's care,
In gardens where our wishes throng,
The language of bloom, a timeless song.

Laughter in the Breeze

Laughter weaves through branches high,
With every gust, it learns to fly,
A joyous chorus, light and free,
Carried forth by nature's glee.

It tickles leaves and stirs the air,
In moments shared, without a care,
With every smile, the world expands,
A dance of hope across the lands.

A New Dawn Unfolds

As night retreats with tender grace,
The dawn arrives to light its space,
Awakening the dreams once bound,
In every heart, a pulse profound.

With colors bright the world ignites,
In whispers soft, the sky invites,
A canvas fresh for life to paint,
A new dawn unfolds, where hope is quaint.

The Rebirth Ritual

In moonlit whispers, the old trees sway,
Awakening spirits from the dreams of clay.
Their roots entwined in the soil of night,
Breathing life into shadows, igniting the light.

With hands outstretched, we gather the stars,
Crafting new worlds from the threads of scars.
The ashes of yesterday rise up and dance,
In the warmth of potential, we embrace the
chance.

Gardens of Tomorrow

Sowing the seeds of a brighter dawn,
In the soil of hope, where the past is drawn.
Petals unfold in a kaleidoscope hue,
Whispers of future in each morning dew.

With every heartbeat, the blossoms arise,
Painting our dreams in the azure skies.
Nature's embrace in a soft, sweet refrain,
Gardens of tomorrow, where love breaks the
chain.

Tides of Vibrance

As the sun dips low, a spectrum ignites,
The ocean waves hum with shimmering lights.
Colors collide in a passionate embrace,
Nature's canvas strokes time and space.

With each ebb and flow, a story unfolds,
In whispers of water, the universe holds.
A symphony crafted from light and sound,
In the tides of vibrance, our souls are unbound.

The Revival of Dreams

In the stillness of night, where silence prevails,
Whispers of dreams drift on soft, gentle gales.
They weave through the cosmos, a luminous
stream,
Embracing the hearts that dare to believe.

With courage as fuel, we shatter the dark,
Igniting the embers, we reignite the spark.
For every lost dream is a chance to reclaim,
In the revival of dreams, we play the same game.

Renewal in the Air

Fresh blooms awaken, colors bold and bright,
Beneath the sun's embrace, they bask in light.
Whispers of the breeze carry tales anew,
As life begins to dance, and skies turn blue.

Each petal hints of promise, soft and sweet,
A tapestry of joy beneath our feet.
In every corner, nature's spirit sings,
Renewal blooms where hope begins to spring.

First Light of Hope

In dawn's first blush, the darkness starts to flee,
As golden rays bring warmth to you and me.
The shadows of the night fade into grace,
Illuminating dreams in their embrace.

With every heartbeat, possibilities arise,
Like butterflies released to greet the skies.
In this gentle moment, futures intertwine,
First light of hope, a promise so divine.

An Ode to the Season

Oh splendid Autumn, with your painted spires,
You drape the earth in warm, embracing fires.
Crisp leaves pirouette, dancing through the air,
A symphony of color, beyond compare.

With harvest moons aglow, and chill winds
sighing,
Each twilight whispers secrets softly flying.
The bounty of the land, a feast so grand,
In nature's heart, we find a hand in hand.

Vibrant Murmurs

In whispered laughter, children run and play,
As sunlight filters through the trees' ballet.
The vibrant murmurs of a lively stream,
Unravel tales of nature's softest dream.

The world awakens, each note crisp and clear,
In every flutter, life's essence draws near.
From rustling leaves to the birds taking flight,
These vibrant murmurs sing of pure delight.

Chirps and Blossoms

In the cradle of dawn, where shadows retreat,
Gentle chirps rise, a melodious greet,
Blossoms unfold in hues soft and bright,
Nature awakens, kissed by morning light.

Petals whisper secrets to the soft breeze,
A dance of colors among the tall trees,
With each note sung, a new tale begins,
Carried by winds, where the day softly spins.

Sowing Seeds of Change

In the heart of the earth, with hands intertwined,
We plant our dreams where the sun brightly
shines,
Each seed a promise, a flicker of hope,
Through storms and the silence, we'll learn how
to cope.

Nurturing visions like seedlings we care,
Watered by courage, and tendered with prayer,
As seasons will shift, and the turmoil will fade,
A garden of futures from sacrifices made.

Essence of Awakening

The dawn breaks softly, as daylight unfurls,
Unveiling the beauty that in silence swirls,
A whisper of life in each dewdrop's glint,
Awakening souls, both faithful and scant.

With every heartbeat, the world comes alive,
In shadows of doubt, hope dares to survive,
Beneath the still night, the stars softly gleam,
Stirring the spirit, igniting the dream.

The Colorful Canvas

Beneath the painter's brush, the world takes flight,

A canvas of colors, bold and bright,
Swirling in chaos, yet in harmony found,
A symphony of hues that knows no bound.

From deep sapphire oceans to emerald trees,
Each stroke tells a story, carried by ease,
In every shade lies a whisper of grace,
A vibrant reminder of life's endless embrace.

Buds of Promise

In the quiet of dawn, where the whispers do play,

Buds unfurl gently, chasing shadows away.
Each petal a dream, a promise in bloom,
Nature's soft laughter dispels all the gloom.

With colors so vibrant, they dance in the light,
A tapestry woven, a wondrous sight.
Each fragrance a story, a moment to share,
In the heart of the garden, love lingers in air.

Ephemeral Sunshine

Beneath the soft clouds, a golden ray peeks,
Whispers of warmth, as the daylight speaks.
Fleeting and fragile, like a soft-spoken sigh,
  Moments of glory, they shimmer and die.

Glistening dew drops, on petals they cling,
Ephemeral beauty, the heart starts to sing.
In the dance of the day, shadows lengthen and
fade,
Yet the memory lingers, in twilight's cascade.

A Canvas of Color

Brush strokes of nature paint the skies fair,
With hues that can awaken, can silence despair.
Fields of wildflowers, a painter's delight,
Each blossom a note in a symphony bright.

Mountains wear crowns of pure snow and of
green,
Rivers run pastel, a flowing machine.
Every sunrise and sunset, a masterpiece grand,
In the canvas of life, where we all take a stand.

The Melody of Chirping

In the hush of the morning, a chorus ignites,
Chirping and fluting, bringing joy to new heights.

Nature's own symphony, sweet songs intertwine,
Echoing softly, like notes on the vine.

With each tiny heartbeat, the rhythm takes flight,
A ballet of voices, a pure delight.
Through branches and leaves, they weave and
they play,
In the melody of chirping, the world finds its way.

Nature's Gentle Nudge

In whispering winds, the trees converse,
Sprouting dreams beneath the universe.
With every rustle, a promise unfolds,
Nature's gentle nudge, a story told.

Mountains rise, clad in a misty veil,
While streams carve the earth, their timeless trail.

Birds sing of dawn, in a symphonic flight,
In harmony's embrace, the world ignites.

Flutters of Transformation

A caterpillar dreams within its cocoon,
While the moon hums softly, a tender tune.
Colors burst forth, like laughter in air,
Flutters of transformation dance everywhere.

Petals unfold in a sun-kissed glow,
A canvas of life, as seasons bestow.
With each vibrant hue, a promise anew,
The cycle continues, forever in view.

Revival in the Orchard

Amidst the branches, where blossoms abound,
Life stirs anew in the warm, fertile ground.
Bees hum a harvest, the fruits start to swell,
Revival in the orchard, a tale to tell.

Sunlight filters through leaves, a golden embrace,

Whispers of nature, an unhurried pace.
With each tender heartbeat, the earth reclaims,
In cyclical rhythm, life calls out names.

Paths of Petals

Winding through gardens, where dreams
intertwine,
Paths of petals lead beneath the pine.
Each step is adorned with fragrance and grace,
A tapestry woven in time and space.

Footsteps dance lightly on nature's canvas,
Whispers of stories carried in blossoms.
Under the sky, where the heart feels at home,
Paths of petals invite souls to roam.

A Symphony of New Life

In the morning light a melody sings,
Soft whispers of joy on the breeze takes wing.
Colors awaken, in a vibrant array,
Nature's own symphony welcomes the day.

With petals unfurling and leaves intertwine,
Every note harmonizes in perfect design.
The rustle of trees, the song of the brook,
A symphony played in the heart of the nook.

The Dance of Daffodils

In gardens aglow, the daffodils sway,
Golden trumpets herald the sun's gentle ray.
They whisper to spring with a vibrant embrace,
In a ballet of warmth, they find their own place.

Their laughter in petals, a delicate show,
Dancing with breezes, to and fro they go.
A celebration of life in a dazzling spin,
In the dance of daffodils, new joys begin.

Nature's Rebirth

As winter recedes with a soft, gentle sigh,
Life stirs in the soil, beneath the blue sky.
A tapestry woven with threads green and gold,
Nature awakens, her stories retold.

With each budding flower, a promise is made,
In the arms of the earth, where shadows once
played.
The whispers of spring brush the chill from the
air,
In the cradle of life, we find hope everywhere.

Fresh Starts in Nature

Beneath the frost lies the promise of spring,
A canvas awaiting the brush of new things.
Birds start to gather, their songs fill the morn,
In the tender embrace of a world newly born.

Streams start to shimmer with laughter and light,
As the darkness of winter gives way to the bright.

Each sunrise a canvas, each sunset a part,
In nature's fresh starts, we find hope in our heart.

The Scent of Potential

In the heart of morning's light,
Dreams take root, eager to ignite.
With every breath, the world unveils,
A tapestry of hopes and trails.

Whispers dance in fragrant air,
Possibilities linger everywhere.
A spark ignites in minds anew,
As visions bloom in vibrant hue.

With every shadow cast away,
Tomorrow's promise finds its way.
In the garden of what could be,
The scent of potential, wild and free.

Chasing dawns with open eyes,
We soar aloft through endless skies.
In every heartbeat, life persists,
Embracing all that still exists.

New Arrivals in the Glen

In the glen where sunlight spills,
New life awakens in rolling hills.
Each bud that beams beneath the dew,
A gentle promise, fresh and true.

Crickets chirp a welcoming song,
To lilting blooms that dance along.
With colors bright, they light the way,
As earth rejoices in spring's bouquet.

Beneath the arch of ancient trees,
The whispers of the wind bring ease.
New arrivals in nature's choir,
Spark imaginations, dreams inspire.

Glancing back at days gone by,
We breathe in deep the summer sigh.
In the glen where wonders blend,
Life begins anew, without end.

Awakening Hues

In the quiet of dawn's embrace,
Colors awaken, find their place.
A palette rich, both bold and bright,
Strokes of magic paint the light.

Golden rays kiss petals wide,
Nature's canvas, our hearts abide.
With every brush, the world transforms,
As beauty in stillness, gently swarms.

Each hue a whisper, soft and clear,
A song of colors we hold dear.
In the kaleidoscope's sweet spin,
We lose ourselves, and then begin.

Awakening hues in morning's glow,
Show us paths we yearn to know.
With every shade, a story we weave,
A tapestry of dreams to believe.

Blooming Whispers

Among the garden, secrets sway,
In blooming whispers, they softly play.
Petals brush against the air,
With every movement, tales they share.

Gentle breezes carry scents,
Of love and life in rich contents.
Each flower speaks of joy and strife,
In every bloom, a story of life.

From buds to blossoms, time unfolds,
Whispers of warmth beneath the cold.
With vibrant hues and tender grace,
They dance in rhythm, find their pace.

In the heart of nature's song,
We find a place where we belong.
With blooming whispers, let us hear,
The language of the earth so dear.

Beneath the Frost

Beneath the frost, a secret stirs,
Whispers of life in frozen slurs,
Each crystal flake, a silenced song,
Nurturing dreams where they belong.

Beneath the white, the pulses beat,
Roots entwined in slumber's seat,
The earth holds close its whispered tales,
Awaiting spring's soft, fragrant gales.

In silent darkness, hope lies deep,
Cradled snug, in winter's keep,
As time unfolds its gentle hand,
Awakening life across the land.

Beneath the frost, a promise brews,
To paint the world in vibrant hues,
The thaw will come, as all things must,
And break the spell of winter's dust.

The Budding World

In early dawn, the world ignites,
With color bursting, the heart delights,
Each bud that blooms with whispered grace,
Unveils the beauty of this place.

The dewdrops cling to petals bright,
Reflecting sun's warm, golden light,
A tender touch, a dance begun,
In nature's arms, two hearts as one.

The branches sway, the breezes sing,
As bees embark on their joyous fling,
A symphony of life unfolds,
With every story that nature holds.

In the budding world, all spirits rise,
As laughter flows beneath the skies,
Each heartbeat echoes, wild and free,
In spring's embrace, find unity.

Lush Awakening

Awake, O garden, from slumber's grip,
As sunbeams fall, let blossoms tip,
The lush green carpet calls us near,
With fragrant scents that fill the air.

Each budding leaf, a tale retold,
Of gentle rains and warmth untold,
In vibrant hues, the canvas spreads,
Where life bursts forth and joy abeds.

The rustling trees share secrets old,
As nature's heart beats brave and bold,
Together, roots entwine and weave,
A tapestry of love to believe.

With every breeze, a thrill of grace,
In lush awakening, find your place,
Embrace the beauty all around,
In this paradise, our souls are found.

Softening Shadows

As daylight wanes and whispers fade,
The softening shadows gently invade,
They stretch and yawn, the soft twilight,
Embracing the stars, igniting the night.

In dusky hues, the world transforms,
A tranquil peace, as stillness warms,
The wind's soft lullaby, sweet and low,
Guides us to dreams where wishes flow.

Beneath the trees, the twilight sighs,
As night descends, the moonlight flies,
With every flicker, a fire glows,
As mysteries of night gently flows.

In softening shadows, hearts entwine,
Where whispers linger, and hopes align,
Let the night cradle each weary soul,
In the embrace of darkness, we feel whole.

Budding Dreams

In twilight's whisper, seeds take flight,
With hopes and wishes cloaked in light.
They stretch and yawn beneath the sky,
Awakening softly, the world awry.

Each dream a petal, unfurling grace,
In every heart, a sacred space.
As dew-kissed mornings dance and twirl,
Budding dreams bloom, a new world's swirl.

Through shadows cast, they push and strive,
A chorus of voices begins to thrive.
From deep in the earth, to sunlight's gleam,
The magic unfolds, it's more than a dream.

With every step on this fragile ground,
The promise of life and love abound.
In gentle hands, the future gleams,
As we nurture our budding dreams.

Canvas of Colors

The dawn breaks forth in hues so bright,
A painter's brush ignites the night.
With splashes bold and strokes divine,
The canvas of colors begins to shine.

Crimson skies of fiery embrace,
Emerald fields in tranquil grace.
Golden rays that dance and play,
A symphony crafted at the break of day.

Amidst the shades, our spirits soar,
In every hue, a tale to explore.
With whispers of violet and indigo seas,
Nature's palette beckons us to seize.

Each moment a stroke, each breath a hue,
In this artwork of life, we find what's true.
From dark to light, we learn to feel,
In the canvas of colors, our souls reveal.

Rebirth in the Meadow

Amidst the whispers of the breeze,
New life emerges, the heart at ease.
Golden daisies in the morning glow,
Rebirth in the meadow, steady and slow.

The brook murmurs secrets to the stones,
While butterflies dance on delicate tones.
With roots entwined in the rich, warm earth,
Spring brings the promise of beauty and birth.

Petals unfurl as the sun ascends,
Each vibrant hue with the joy it sends.
In every crevice where shadows play,
The meadow awakens, chasing night away.

Together we stand where the wildflowers sway,
In moments of stillness, the heart learns to pray.
For in nature's embrace, we find our way,
A rebirth in the meadow, come what may.

Gentle Thaw

Winter's breath begins to wane,
As gentle thaw releases chain.
The icy grasp on branches bare,
A soft release, the promise in the air.

Snowdrops peek through layers of white,
While crocus blooms in morning light.
With every drop from thawing eaves,
A symphony sung as nature believes.

The world awakens, life to renew,
In silken threads of emerald hue.
As whispers of warmth sweep through the trees,
Time gently nudges the heart to seize.

From frozen dreams to flowing streams,
Nature unfolds its softest themes.
In the gentle thaw, we find our grace,
A tender touch in an ever-changing space.

The Great Unfolding

In shadows cast by dawn's first light,
The whispers of the world ignite,
Each moment swells with silent grace,
As time unveils its hidden face.

From seed to bloom, the journey wends,
Through trials faced, and mending bends,
The fabric of our lives entwines,
In patterns deep where fate designs.

With every breath, the past recedes,
While futures pulse like ancient seeds,
We walk the path where dreams collide,
In the great unfolding, side by side.

So let us dance in sacred spheres,
Embracing joy, releasing fears,
For in this world of ebb and flow,
The great unfolding starts to show.

Verses of Emergence

In the quiet depths of weary night,
Awakens the dawn, a whispering light,
From cocooned dreams the soul will rise,
With wings unbound, we touch the skies.

The pulse of life in veins does sing,
As fervor mounts with the breath of spring,
Each verse a note, each heartbeat a chord,
In symphonies of souls, our spirits soared.

Like rivers flowing, we carve our place,
Emerging from doubt, with steadfast grace,
Together we weave our stories profound,
In the verses of emergence, hope is found.

So let us gather, hearts aflame,
With voices united, no two the same,
In this tapestry of life, we'll weave,
Verses of love, where all can believe.

Nature's Sweet Symphony

Beneath the boughs of ancient trees,
A melody dances on the breeze,
The rustling leaves in harmony sway,
As nature sings her sweet ballet.

The brook's soft laughter, the call of the dove,
Compose a song of peace and love,
In every petal and every stone,
A symphony echoes, we're never alone.

The sun dips low, painting skies in gold,
As twilight whispers stories untold,
In the hush of night, the stars appear,
Notes of the universe fill the sphere.

So take a moment, breathe it in,
Join nature's chorus, let life begin,
For in each heartbeat, the world will see,
The sweetest symphony, just you and me.

Treading on Fresh Earth

Upon the soil, where life takes flight,
We tread with care, in morning light,
With each step forward, new paths unfold,
Stories of courage and dreams untold.

The scent of rain, the kiss of dew,
Awakens the heart, inviting the new,
In every footprint, a legacy sown,
On fresh earth, the seeds of tomorrow are grown.

The whispers of nature, the wisdom it gives,
Reminds us all of how beauty lives,
In every corner, both wild and tame,
Join the dance of life, call out our name.

So let us wander, let us explore,
Discover the miracles waiting in store,
For as we walk on this sacred ground,
Treading on fresh earth, our souls are found.

The Colors of Change

Leaves turn to gold in the crisp autumn air,
Whispers of summer fading, a moment so rare.
Nature's brush paints a canvas alive,
With every stroke, the seasons strive.

Breezes carry stories, secrets untold,
In the rhythm of time, watch the world unfold.
From birth to decay, a vibrant dance,
Embracing the cycle, we join in the trance.

Winter's chill whispers, a lullaby's song,
Yet underneath the frost, life waits to be strong.
Emerging anew when the warmth reappears,
A reminder of beauty, through laughter and tears.

Reflections in a Puddle

After the rain, a world upside down,
Clouds drift in silence, a soft, silver crown.
Each droplet captures, the sky's gentle sigh,
Mirrors of moments, as time passes by.

Children jump in, with laughter and splashes,
Creating new ripples, where stillness once dashes.

Each reflection a memory, framed by the light,
In puddles of wonder, everything feels right.

A dance of the raindrops, a rhythm so sweet,
Covering sidewalks with nature's heartbeat.
In these fleeting images, we pause and we see,
The beauty of life's delicate tapestry.

The Joy of First Blooms

In a quiet garden, where winter once laid,
Awakening blossoms begin to cascade.
Petals unfurling, each a vibrant hue,
Whispers of springtime, a promise renewed.

Bees hum a tune, as they dance from each stem,
Gathering nectar, life's sweet diadem.
Sunlight spills gently, a warm embrace found,
In the arms of the flowers, where beauty abounds.

Joy bursts like laughter, in colors so bright,
Transforming the earth, with exquisite delight.
Each bloom tells a story, of hope and of cheer,
A canvas of life, inviting us near.

Chasing Sunbeams

In fields of gold, where the daisies sway,
Children run wild, chasing dreams every day.
Sunbeams embrace them, with warmth on their
skin,
A race against shadows, let the laughter begin.

Butterflies flutter, as if caught in a dance,
Each color a whisper, a moment's romance.
Laughter echoes softly beneath the vast sky,
In the arms of the sunshine, we learn how to fly.

As dusk draws near, painting skies with fire,
The day holds its breath, fulfilling our desire.
In the chase of the light, we find our own way,
Among the sunbeams, forever we'll play.

The Call of the Wild

In the heart of the forest, where silence sings,
Beneath ancient trees, the wild spirit clings.
Whispers of freedom in the rustling leaves,
A symphony beckons, as the wild heart believes.

Mountains stand watch with their towering grace,

Echoes of creatures that vanish without trace.
The wind carries tales of the brave and the bold,
Of lives intertwined in the warmth of the cold.

A brook bursts in laughter through stones worn
with age,
The canvas of nature reveals a wise page.
With each breath of the earth, our souls
intertwine,
In the call of the wild, we are destined to shine.

So venture, dear wanderer, into the embrace,
Where wilderness thrives, and time knows no
space.
Listen to the heartbeat that pulses your way,
In the call of the wild, forever we'll stay.

Echoes of the Awakening

As dawn spills its colors on slumbering ground,
The echoes of morning are gentle and profound.
Birds serenade softly, in melodies sweet,
Nature's own choir, where hearts and skies meet.

The dew on the petals, like jewels, shines bright,
A whisper of hope in the soft morning light.
Each creature stirs slowly, from dreams yet
untold,
In the echoes of awakening, new stories unfold.

The trees shake off shadows, embrace the sun's
ray,
While rivers hum softly, inviting the day.
In this tranquil moment, we witness the birth,
Of the miracles weaving the fabric of earth.

So listen, dear friend, to the sweet, sacred sound,
Of echoes arising, where beauty is found.
Let the morning awaken the dreams that you
keep,
In the dance of the day, join the world as it leaps.

Nature's Reclamation

From the cracks in the pavement, green sprouts arise,
Nature's soft whispers, beneath bruised skies.
With patience and courage, she claims her domain,
In the dance of resilience, she whispers our name.

Vines wrap around ruins, and wildflowers bloom,

In the faces of man, nature overcomes gloom.
She writes on the walls of the forgotten and worn,

A story of life, where new dreams are born.

The rivers run clear, through ashes and stone,
A testament born from the seeds we have sown.
With every twig snapping, a promise resounds,
That nature will flourish, in spite of our bounds.

So honor her presence, this canvas so vast,
For in nature's reclamation, our futures are cast.
Let us learn from her wisdom, as seasons unfold,
In the heart of her wildness, find stories untold.

Waking the Slumbering Earth

In the hush of the twilight, the earth holds her
breath,
While stars weave their stories of life, love, and
death.
Yet beneath the soft blanket of frost and of night,

The slumbering earth stirs, preparing for light.

The moon cradles secrets, in silvered embrace,
As shadows grow deeper, and time slows its pace.

But soon, with the dawn, there will come a great
call,
Waking the slumbering earth, reviving us all.

Roots stretch and deepen, breaking ground with a
sigh,
As petals unfurl, greeting the sky.
From whispers of dreams to vibrant displays,
The earth, once asleep, is now waking to play.

So gather the moments, take heed of the day,
For life thrives in cycles, like night turns to May.
In the dance of the seasons, let our spirits take
flight,
Waking the slumbering earth, into radiant light.

Whirlwind of Blossoms

In a dance of petals, colors collide,
Whispers of spring, love's gentle guide.
Around the soft breeze, the blossoms twine,
Nature's canvas painted, in shades divine.

Daffodils bow, while the tulips sway,
A whirlwind of blossoms, brightens the day.
In gardens alive, where the heart can see,
Fragments of beauty, wild and free.

Rustling leaves join in, a soft serenade,
In this playful ballet, worries do fade.
From the roots to the sky, life's vibrant spark,
On this journey of colors, we leave our mark.

Hold the moment close, as time starts to fly,
In this whirlwind of blossoms, we learn to fly.
Let laughter and love weave their sweet refrain,
For in every petal, joy shall remain.

The Awakening Heart

In the hush of dawn, a whispering sigh,
Shadows retreat, as day begins to fly.
With each gentle heartbeat, colors arise,
The world awakens, under softening skies.

Flowers unfurl, like dreams from the night,
Their fragrance entices, a pure delight.
In a symphony of whispers, hope takes its part,
Harmony blooms in the awakening heart.

The sun spills its gold on the dew-kissed ground,
Every moment precious, in beauty we're bound.
As the light gently dances, embracing the day,
In the warmth of connection, we find our way.

With open arms, and spirits set free,
Each heartbeat a promise, each breath a decree.
Together forever, as new journeys start,
In the vessel of time, we nurture the heart.

Nature's Happy Footprints

Across gentle hills, where the wildflowers sway,
Nature whispers softly, guiding our way.
Every footprint tells a tale of the past,
In the realm of the green, memories cast.

Through meadows and streams, adventure
unfolds,
Wrapped in the warmth that nature beholds.
With laughter like echoes, in the crisp, cool air,
Nature's embrace, a love beyond compare.

The rustle of leaves, a dance in the trees,
Nature sings out, an anthem with ease.
From mountain to valley, joy's path intertwines,
In the heart of this world, a legacy shines.

So let us roam freely, amongst the wild things,
In nature's grand canvas, our spirit takes wings.
With every simple moment, adventure awaits,
In nature's happy footprints, love resonates.

Breathing in Harmony

In the stillness of night, where the stars softly
gleam,
The universe whispers, unraveling dreams.
With every deep breath, we weave and align,
In melodies sweet, our souls intertwine.

Through valleys of shadows, we find the bright
signs,
In the rhythm of life, all the love aligns.
From the mountains' high peaks to the rivers that
flow,
Breathing in harmony, let the connections grow.

Each sigh of the earth, a song to be heard,
Echoes of wisdom in whispers of bird.
In the dance of the cosmos, our essence we share,

Breathing together, we rise, pure and rare.

So linger in silence, let the heart's song play,
In this symphony of life, let love find its way.
With each tender moment, unfold and explore,
Breathing in harmony, we awaken once more.

Awakening Blooms

In early light, the petals sigh,
A tapestry of colors, reaching high.
The soft caress of morning dew,
Each blossom opens, fresh and new.

Amidst the green, a vibrant hue,
The earth awakens, life anew.
Like dreams that break the night's old spell,
In fragrant whispers, peace does dwell.

Beneath the sun, they stretch, they yearn,
For every bud a heart that burns.
With gentle winds, they sway and dance,
In nature's grasp, they find romance.

So let us breathe this fragrant air,
In every bloom, the promise rare.
For life in cycle turns and grows,
Awakening blooms, sweet as a rose.

The Whisper of Fresh Starts

In twilight's hush, a vow is born,
Where shadows fade, and hope is sworn.
The night retreats; the dawn arrives,
In every heart, a fresh start thrives.

With every breath, we cast away,
The weight of yesterday's dismay.
In whispered dreams, we find our light,
A path unfolds, so bold, so bright.

The stars above begin to wane,
As sunlight pours through every vein.
With every pulse, we rise anew,
Embracing what we thought we knew.

So take a step, unleash your soul,
For in this moment, we are whole.
The world awaits your shining spark,
In whispers soft, ignite the dark.

Sunlit Renewal

Upon the dawn, the golden rays,
Awaken dreams from night's deep haze.
A canvas bright, the sky's embrace,
In sunlight's kiss, we find our place.

With every beam, a story spins,
Washing over where the heart begins.
The warmth of hope, it fills the air,
In every glance, a promise fair.

The flowers nod, they drink the light,
As shadows flee before the bright.
Each moment glows, a chance to thrive,
In sunlit fields, we feel alive.

So let us bask in this renewal,
Embrace the dawn, our hearts, the fuel.
For every day brings forth the chance,
To dance with joy, to leap, to prance.

Dance of the Daffodils

In fields of gold, they sway and spin,
The daffodils, where joys begin.
A symphony of springtime cheer,
With every turn, they draw us near.

Their golden faces smile with grace,
In the gentle breeze, a sweet embrace.
With laughter in the sunlight bright,
They dance together, pure delight.

As if the earth has found its song,
In rhythmic sways, they move along.
Each petal twirls, a light-hearted tune,
Together beneath the warming moon.

So join the dance, let spirits thrive,
In daffodil fields, we'll come alive.
With nature's rhythm, hearts unchained,
In every step, pure joy regained.

Milton Keynes UK
Ingram Content Group UK Ltd.
UKHW032036191024
449814UK00010B/475